WHAT EVERY STUDENT SHOULD KNOW ABOUT USING A HANDBOOK

Kim Murray
University of South Florida

PEARSON
Longman

New York   San Francisco   Boston
London   Toronto   Sydney   Tokyo   Singapore   Madrid
Mexico City   Munich   Paris   Cape Town   Hong Kong   Montreal

Executive Editor: Lynn M. Huddon
Development Manager: Mary Ellen Curley
Development Editor: Michael Greer
Executive Marketing Manager: Megan Galvin-Fak
Production Manager: Stacey Kulig
Project Coordination, Text Design, and Electronic Page Makeup: Pre-Press PMG
Senior Designer: Sue Kinney
Cover Illustration: Veer Images
Senior Manufacturing Buyer: Roy Pickering
Printer and Binder: Courier Corporation/Stoughton
Cover Printer: Courier Corporation/Stoughton

Cataloging-in-Publication Data on file with the Library of Congress.

Please visit us at www.ablongman.com

ISBN 13: 978-0-205-56384-5
ISBN 10: 0-205-56384-8

2 3 4 5 6 7 8 9 10—CRS—10 09 08 07

CONTENTS

PREFACE

Have you ever really taken the time to get to know your handbook? How often are you encouraged to bring your handbook to class, open it up, and see what's in there? Do you experience frustration when you do need to look something up? Do you close the book in despair and turn to the Web for answers? *What Every Student Should Know About Using a Handbook* is written for you, the college writer. We hope it leads you to a better understanding of what your handbook offers, how to make better use of it, and how to develop a better relationship with it in the interests of improving your writing.

Longman publishes a number of handbooks, and they're all different. Writing, composition, and rhetoric are diverse and dynamic fields, and there's no one right way to learn to write more effectively. So handbooks tend to take different approaches, and some of them vary widely in organization and layout. Nonetheless, there are some common elements that all handbooks cover.

What Every Student Should Know About Using a Handbook is designed so that it can be used in tandem with any Longman handbook. Its focus is on the core topics and strategies that apply broadly to any handbook and to any writing project. Its five chapters are designed to

- help you understand the uses of your handbook;
- teach you how to navigate your handbook to find the information you need;
- acquaint you with the kind of help your handbook provides;
- show you how using your handbook can strengthen your writing in any setting; and
- introduce you to the ways your handbook can guide you through writing a formal research paper.

The exercises and activities included here are intended to encourage you to take a closer look at your handbook. The Appendix presents a sample student paper with annotations that illustrate common writing pitfalls and explain how using your handbook can help you avoid them.

We hope you learn something new, and discover more helpful, less frustrating ways of using your handbook. Overall, *What Every Student Should Know About Using a Handbook* will introduce you to one of the most underrated tools you'll ever buy and hopefully prepare you to make the best possible use of it.

1

WHY DO I NEED THIS BOOK?

It feels a little strange to be reading one book that tells you how to read another one, doesn't it? This is probably a whole new idea for you. But think of it this way: If you weren't a skilled mechanic, would you start tinkering under the hood of your car without a repair manual? Probably not. So why would you begin your college career without knowing how to use your "writing repair manual"— your handbook? Here's another way to think of it: If you're like most people, you learn to use a new software tool (like a word processor or a photo editor) by diving in and playing around with it for a while to see how it works. But at some point, you probably run into a question you can't answer, and so you decide to consult the user's guide or the help menu. Think of this book as the user's guide for your handbook. Dive into your handbook, flip its pages, browse around for a while, and then when you get stuck or confused, consult this book to learn more about your handbook's features and functions. You may be surprised at how much a handbook can really help you when it comes to writing papers for college courses.

Handbooks may be the most misunderstood resources available to college students—and the most valuable. Most handbooks seem overwhelming—too many sections, chapters, rules, and lists; too many documentation guides; too much information. But once you understand how to use it, you may never want to let your handbook disappear from your shelf—not just while you're in college, but for many years to come. In fact, you may never again find so much useful information in one place.

So why do you need this book? Some writing students admit to being intimidated by grammar and punctuation. They assume that handbooks focus only on grammar, so the logical assumption is that handbooks are intimidating, too. Often, students just never take the time to understand what handbooks really offer, assuming that they can find everything they need on the Internet. And too much of the time, professors require a handbook but never make assignments from it, so you have no real way of knowing why you were required to buy it. You may feel like you've been left to figure out when and how to use your handbook without much guidance or class discussion at all. As a result, too many handbooks remain parked on the shelf, misunderstood and under-appreciated.

Longman publishers hopes that this guide, *What Every Student Should Know About Using a Handbook,* will prevent a book you've spent good money on from gathering dust.

Just What *Is* a Handbook, Anyway?

If someone asked you, "What is a handbook?," which of the following answers would you choose?

a) a collection of short stories, essays, and poems for English class
b) a calendar, like a course planner
c) a book students use like a thesaurus
d) an alphabetical text like an encyclopedia that lists common terms students use in English courses
e) a resource for writing, research, and grammar
f) none of the above

If you're not sure of your answer, then you may understand why we published this book. Often, students are required to purchase a handbook in their first-year composition courses, and then the instructor rarely refers to it again. You never get to know it. This little book is designed to help you do just that—to understand this remarkable resource, which may just be the most valuable book you buy while you're in college. (By the way, the correct answer is "e" . . . but keep reading.)

Throughout your education, you may have used a variety of reference books: an atlas, an almanac, a thesaurus, a dictionary. Each of these resources is different from your college handbook. To find out more about how your handbook compares to other reference books, look at the table below and then answer the questions in Exercise 1.1.

Atlas	A collection of charts and/or maps, generally geographical. Atlases also sometimes illustrate anatomy, astronomy, or other natural sciences.
Almanac	A collection of lists, charts, tables, important dates, and short articles associated with a specific field of interest. Most common are historical almanacs, but almanacs also cover topics ranging from farming to sports.
Dictionary	An alphabetic catalog of precise word definitions. If you don't know what a word means, use a dictionary to look it up.
Thesaurus	A collection of words, providing words with similar meaning as well as cross-references, making synonyms easy to find. If you have been repeating the same word in an essay and want to look for a synonym to use instead, check a thesaurus.
Handbook	A comprehensive guidebook to the entire process of writing correctly, from prewriting and composing through preparing a final document. Handbooks also include conventions of grammar and style, guidance for doing research including documentation style guides, and a wealth of other information that you will find useful in academic writing. Most handbooks also offer guidance for writing other kinds of documents, including resumes, web pages, and presentations.

■ EXERCISE 1.1: What IS a Handbook?

How does a handbook compare to other reference books? Indicate whether each of the following statements is True or False.

T   F   1. A handbook includes information about writing as well as grammar.

T   F   2. A handbook is like a dictionary; everything is organized alphabetically.

T   F   3. I would look in my handbook for a list of some of the abbreviations my teacher writes in the margins of my paper.

T   F   4. My handbook would be a good place to find information about the current population of Colorado.

T   F   5. My handbook would be a good resource for me if I wanted to spell "accommodate."

T   F   6. My handbook includes information about how to cite sources in research papers.

T   F   7. I would use a thesaurus, rather than a handbook, to find synonyms for the word "talk."

T   F   8. My handbook includes a sample student paper with teacher comments.

T   F   9. My handbook lists information about what courses are required for my major and how many credits I need to graduate.

T   F   10. My handbook offers some advice on how to write introductions and conclusions.

And What's *In* a Handbook?

Now that you have some idea of what a handbook is, let's look a little more closely at what it includes. If you assume that your handbook has a wealth of information about grammar, you are certainly correct. What you may not know, however, is that it's really a comprehensive guide to the entire writing process. And writing tasks don't stop once you finish your freshman composition course—or even once you've finished all your college course work and graduated. If you really get comfortable with it, then chances are you will want to keep your college handbook after you graduate. A handbook is a handy reference for information you'll need as you start a career—information about how to compose a job application letter and format a resume, for example—and information you'll need in almost any job you take—how to write concisely, for example, or organize a report. Your handbook will let you look up grammar principles that many people tend to forget—such as when to use *affect* or *effect, than* or *then, its* or *it's.* But before your college handbook can become a symbol of success in first-year English and effective writing in the years beyond, it will need to be opened and used.

To get started—even though you could no doubt figure out how to use your handbook on your own—here's a good activity for getting to know what's available inside it. Exercise 1.2—the Scavenger Hunt below—will help you dive in, explore your handbook, and see how easy it is to use.

■ **EXERCISE 1.2: Scavenger Hunt**
To answer the following questions, use all the resources your handbook provides: the inside front and back covers, the index, the tabs (if you are using a tabbed handbook), colored pages or borders on pages, the various tables of contents. List page numbers and provide specific answers for each question.

1. If your teacher tells you that you need to work on creating *better structure* or *organization* for your essay, what parts of your handbook would offer you the most help?

2. In what chapter would you find information about writing *thesis statements*?

3. Where can you find a list of the symbols and abbreviations a teacher might use to write comments and notes in the margins of your paper?

4. Where can you find information about when to use the pronouns *I* and *me*? (Ex. "Tim gave the algebra book to John and _____.")

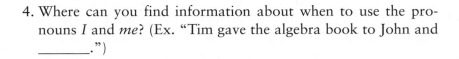

5. If you're not sure about the function of a *semicolon,* what parts of your handbook show you how to use one?

_____

6. Where would you look to find out the difference between an *adjective* and an *adverb*?

_____

7. If you're not sure how to use visuals in your writing assignments, which section of your handbook would you turn to?

_____

8. Where would you look in your handbook if you need to prepare for an upcoming *essay exam*?

_____

9. If you want to work on your phrasing or improve the *style* of your writing, what pages provide the most suggestions?

_____

10. Where would you look in your handbook if you need help *choosing a research topic*?

_____

How Are Handbooks Organized?

By now it should be clear: Your handbook is a reference tool that is specifically designed to help you improve your writing in every situation. Whether your handbook is a big hardcover book, a smaller book with a spiral binding, a tiny pocket guidebook, or an online resource, the information it contains generally falls into three major topic areas, all critically important for academic writers: **1) writing, 2) research,** and **3) grammar, punctuation, and mechanics.** (In the context of research and composing, mechanics refers to the details of writing that go along with grammar and punctuation including capitalization, underlining, italics, spelling, and similar topics.)

The organization of handbooks commonly matches the flow of how most writers move through the writing process. The early chapters usually explore ways to write clearly and cohesively, and how to plan, draft, and revise an essay. Often these chapters also include information about reading critically, since this is often an important skill for writing well. The middle section of most handbooks includes chapters on choosing and narrowing a topic, finding and evaluating sources, appropriate use of those sources, and citing information correctly for research papers. The later chapters usually focus on grammar and style, punctuation, and mechanics. Some handbooks put grammar and style earlier, but the order suggested above is the most typical.

Where handbooks differ is in how much information they offer for each of the three main areas, and how many additional topics they include. Although you will sometimes hear that all handbooks are the same, the reality is that they are often quite different: Some emphasize writing in other disciplines beyond freshman composition; some include extensive information about professional writing; some are barebones and focus almost exclusively on grammar and documentation. Content varies from one to the next.

Handbooks also come in many different shapes and sizes: comprehensive hardcover and softcover books; "brief" (although some would dispute that label) comb- or spiral bound versions, usually with tabbed dividers, and often with or without exercises; pocket versions that include only the most basic information; or online ebooks. For more extensive research and writing information, many handbook publishers also offer extensive websites with a wide range of other resources, including videos, interactive grammar tutorials, and quizzes. Check the preface and back cover of your handbook to see if there is an online version or other online resources you can use with your handbook.

Online Handbooks

Many print handbooks are available as ebooks, but there are also handbooks that exist only online, without a print version. Internet-based handbooks differ considerably from print versions. These online resources can be convenient, and if you know what key areas or search terms to use, the information you need appears on the screen in less time than it would take to find the same thing in a book.

However, internet handbooks can't come to class with you, so anything you might want to find out in class will have to wait until you're back at your computer. And you need to be very clear about how your questions or issues are categorized. Are you having difficulties with sentence parts, or with punctuation and mechanics? Would your question fall under "Common Sentence Problems," or under "Advanced Sentence Concepts"? Do you need help narrowing a topic? How would you search for this? On the whole, a print and online combination might be the better choice for your handbook. A print book can stay on your shelf forever; it's hard to say how long an online handbook will be available to you.

Other Resources

If you are using this booklet, you are probably using a handbook published by Longman, a division of Pearson Education. Longman offers an online resource called *MyCompLab* packaged at no additional cost with all its handbooks. If your handbook did not come with access to *MyCompLab,* you can go online (www.mycomplab.com) and purchase individual access.

MyCompLab is organized into three areas: grammar, writing, and research. Under grammar, you'll find online diagnostic tests that allow you to find out whether you need refresher courses in any areas of grammar, style, or usage. Then, after you target your strengths and weaknesses, you can use the practice exercises in ExerciseZone to build your skill level in grammar, mechanics, punctuation, and style. You can also watch a series of Macromedia Flash movies that illustrate the "Top 20" grammar errors students often make and ways to fix them. Using voiceover and animation, each video focuses on only one grammatical issue at a time. As you watch the short videos, you see more than one example so that you can apply what you learn to your own writing. The writing section of *MyCompLab* includes a wealth of writing prompts and a tutorial on the writing process, and the research section offers tutorials on the research process and avoiding plagiarism, as well as access to a wide variety of academic and journalistic databases.

Exchange is a peer review program within *MyCompLab* that provides opportunities for you to share your paper with other students so that they can respond to your work.

■ **EXERCISE 1.3: What's In *My* Handbook?**

Now that you know that your handbook is divided into three main content areas (writing, research, and grammar and punctuation), look at the detailed table of contents (probably at the front or back of your handbook) and list the main topics you see covered in each section.

Does your list show anything beyond the three main topics? What additional content does your handbook have? What might that tell you about the way your professor may approach your freshman composition course?

_____

_____

_____

_____

_____

_____

_____

_____

_____

_____

■ **EXERCISE 1.4: How Well Do I Know My Handbook Now?**

Using your handbook, answer True or False to the following statements.

T   F   1. The inside front cover provides an overview of the book.

T   F   2. If my teacher marks a "cs" in the margin of my paper, I have no convenient place in the handbook to find out what that means.

T   F   3. My handbook has grammar exercises.

T   F   4. The research paper citation information is the same for all of my courses.

T   F   5. There is color-coding on the inside cover to show me the different areas my handbook covers.

T   F   6. My handbook includes information about writing essay exams.

T   F   7. I could consult my handbook to find information about using commas—and I could use its website to find more exercises about commas.

T   F   8. The rules for using capital letters appear in the section of my handbook titled "Mechanics."

T   F   9. Chapters on writing in courses other than English appear in my handbook.

T   F   10. My handbook offers chapters on vocabulary building.

Now you're ready to go!

2

HOW DO I FIND THE INFORMATION I NEED?

Handbooks can be overwhelming. The amount of information they present is both wide and deep. How do you find what you need when you need it? Well, most handbooks provide a range of tools to help you with this task. If you did Exercise 1.2, the Scavenger Hunt, in Chapter 1, you probably already discovered some of these. Rather than diving into your handbook and flipping pages in an attempt to find something by chance, let's take some time now to explore the tools in your handbook that are designed to make your search process more efficient and ultimately successful.

- **Inside covers:** This is the first place to look if you need to find information quickly. Handbooks often have either brief or complete contents listed on these inside covers, either back or front. Handbook contents are typically organized using an alphanumeric (letters plus numbers) code. For example, the first part or chapter may have several sections listed as 1a. Subject, 1b. Purpose, 1c. Audience, and so on. You can use these alphanumeric codes to find the specific topics you need.
- **Index:** The index, located in the back of your handbook, is one of the most important places to look in order to find specific information quickly. Information in the index is listed alphabetically by topic, with a list of the page numbers where that topic is treated. If your teacher mentions a word or topic in class and you aren't sure of the meaning, try looking in the index.

- **Running heads/feet:** The text at the top (heads) or bottom (feet) of each page function like a heading in an outline. Generally, handbook headers and footers include the section number and the topic covered in that section. If you get lost looking for information, flip through to find an appropriate heading, and then back up to the beginning of the chapter.
- **Divider tabs:** If your handbook has tabs, they will direct you quickly to the main parts of the book (writing process, research, grammar, and punctuation, for example) so you can flip directly to them, without stopping to refer to the table of contents. Many handbook tabs also include a table of contents for that section, with page or chapter references. Look on the back side of each tab to see what that section covers.
- **Revision guide (or editing symbols, or proofreading symbols):** Most handbooks include this valuable list, which will help you interpret the notations your teacher makes on your papers. If you aren't sure what a teacher's marginal note—for example, "CS"—means, check the revision guide. In this case, the guide would tell you that "CS" means comma splice. Even more important, the revision guide will refer you to sections of the handbook that offer helpful suggestions about how to fix the errors your teacher notes.

ACTIVITY: TABBING YOUR HANDBOOK

At the beginning of your composition course, use Post-Its to mark sections of your handbook that seem like they might be most useful. Even if your handbook already has tabs, create your own customized "tabbed" version, based on what looks valuable to you personally. Write abbreviations for the topics covered on your Post-Its. Then, throughout your composition course, whenever you find yourself using a section of your handbook, mark it with a Post-It.

Do your new tabs match up with your original ones? Were you right when you thought that certain sections would prove most useful—or are you finding that things you hadn't anticipated are actually more important?

Here is a list of some commonly referenced topics you might want to tab in your own handbook:

In this section of your handbook	Listed in the table of contents as . . .	Write this on your Post-It
WRITING	Thesis statement	Thesis
	Outline format	Outlines
	Strategies for drafting	Drafts
	Commonly used transitions	Transitions
	Introductions and conclusions	Intros & concls
	Strategies for revising/rewriting	Rewriting
	Sample business letter	Business letter
	Sample résumé	Résumé
RESEARCH	MLA documentation	MLA
	MLA works-cited format	WC
	MLA sample paper	Paper format
	Avoiding plagiarism	Plagiarism
GRAMMAR & PUNCTUATION	Literary present tense	Present tense
	First person "I"	"I"
	Often-confused words	WW
	Sexist language	Sexist lang.
	Using commas correctly	Commas
	Quotation Marks	" "
	Other Punctuation	Punct.
	Writing essay exams	Essay exams
OTHER RESOURCES	Glossary	Glossary
	Index	Index
	Editing symbols	Symbols

■ **EXERCISE 2.1: Navigating My Handbook**

Below is a list of topics you might encounter as you write papers for your classes. Try to find at least two navigational aids for locating the pages in your book that provide information about each of the following topics. On the lines provided, write where you found these aids (index, inside cover, etc.).

1. **Comma splices.** This is one of the most frequent errors that writers make.

   _____   _____

2. **Sentence fragments.** If you're not sure what a fragment is, you might also want to learn more about subordinate—or dependent—clauses.

   _____   _____

3. **Topic sentences.** Find a definition for a topic sentence. Find how a topic sentence relates to a thesis statement.

   _____   _____

4. **Avoiding passive voice.** Overuse of passive voice leads to excessive use of "is/are/was/were" and weakens the power of your writing. Would you look in the writing section or grammar section for information on this? What aids will answer this question?

   _____   _____

5. **A directory to the documentation and citation style(s) required in your class.** This section can streamline the process of preparing your bibliography or works cited page.

   _____   _____

6. **Writing an introduction.** Find the section that offers tips for writing introductions.

   _____   _____

7. **Using an apostrophe before or after the _s_.** Apostrophe errors are among the most frequent mistakes students make in their writing.

   _____   _____

8. **Confusing words (such as they're, there, their).** Many students are uncertain about which "homonym" to use, but your handbook can usually help you understand the differences between them.

   _____   _____

9. **Writing thesis statements.** Find guidelines for what makes a good thesis, and whether you need one for every essay you write.

   _____   _____

10. **Understanding the audience for your writing.** Did you know that *who* you are writing for is as critical as *what* you are writing?

   _____   _____

3

WHAT DOES A
HANDBOOK OFFER?

We have been talking about the three categories of information most handbooks typically cover: writing, research, and grammar. But don't be fooled into thinking that these three categories are separate and unrelated—or into thinking that good academic writing (or a good business letter, or a good website) is an uncomplicated piece of work, consisting only of these three discrete elements. On the contrary, a writing project is one of the most complex tasks you'll face in college. And writing well is a process that weaves together each of the three major areas in a complex, integrated pattern until the end result becomes relatively seamless.

Let's begin by digging in to each section a little deeper and reflecting on why your handbook is arranged the way it is.

The Writing Process

The sections of your handbook on writing instruction guide you by helping you explore components of writing that may not be included in the assignment description itself. For example, you might read about how to brainstorm a topic, narrow a subject, organize your ideas, write a thesis statement, write a first draft, provide adequate support in your paragraphs, or appeal to a specific kind of reader. You'll also find useful ideas about writing introductions and conclusions—among the most important and challenging parts of any document. Although you may hear about some of these things in class, you can look in your handbook for points you may have forgotten or missed.

ACTIVITY: JUST WHAT IS THE WRITING PROCESS?

How do you write? Spend a few minutes thinking about the strongest memories you have of writing. They might be from a high school English class, or even from elementary school. Are your memories related to a particular teacher or classroom? What are some of the "rules" you learned about writing before you came to college? Were you taught to brainstorm first? To make an outline? To edit each section as you write, or to wait until you've completed the piece to edit and revise?

Now jot down the steps you follow when you write. Try to capture your own process as clearly as possible.

When you have completed your list of steps, look at the inside front cover or table of contents of your handbook. Does your process follow the steps outlined in your handbook? How does it differ? Do you think your handbook might provide some useful advice for thinking more about *process* as you write for college?

Your handbook's section on writing process can be especially valuable in helping you take a complicated or lengthy writing project and break it down into manageable steps. Successful writers are not necessarily genetically pre-programmed to write well; instead, they have learned to take a big task, break it down, and take it step by step. You can learn to do this, too, by looking at how your handbook presents an overview of the steps involved in a writing project. At its most basic level, any writing project involves planning and preparing, drafting, revising, and polishing. The biggest mistake any writer can make is to try to go directly from a blank screen to a final paper in one big crunch. It's much more efficient, and ultimately effective, to rough out an outline, then compose a quick draft, and then go back to revise and clarify the finer points. Look for the section of your handbook that deals with this process and explore how it can help you to gain a big-picture perspective on your writing projects and to manage your time more effectively.

No doubt it's pretty clear to you now that writing is not simply the act of putting your thoughts down on paper. Your handbook probably offers a number of strategies for getting started with your writing—freewriting, brainstorming, clustering, and more—as well as finding and narrowing a topic, revising, editing, and creating a final document. Your professor may not take you through each of these steps—but your handbook will.

■ **EXERCISE 3.1: Defining Terms in the Writing Process**

Do you distinguish among drafting, revising, editing, and proofreading? Write your own definition of each term. Now check the index to find the definitions of these terms included in your handbook. How close are they to yours? Do the handbook definitions give you food for thought about the writing process?

My definition of *drafting* is _____

_____.

My handbook's definition of *drafting* is _____

_____.

My definition of *revising* is _____

_____.

My handbook's definition of *revising* is _____

_____.

My definition of *editing* is _____

_____.

My handbook's definition of *editing* is _____

_____.

My definition of *proofreading* is _____

_____.

My handbook's definition of *proofreading* is _____

_____.

Understanding Audience and Purpose

The process of writing is important—understanding that all good writing is really rewriting. Also critically important to good writing are a sense of *audience* and *purpose*. Knowing who you are writing for—your professor? your classmates? yourself?—and knowing what you are trying to accomplish in your writing will help you become a more successful writer. Your handbook may provide strategies for thinking more about this.

■ EXERCISE 3.2: Exploring Audience and Purpose

Check your handbook's navigational aids to find your handbook's discussion of audience and purpose.

1. In what section does this discussion appear? What page numbers? What else is included along with audience and purpose?

_____

2. Does your handbook use a graphic to represent the writing situation or task? What are the main parts of this graphic? How might this graphic help you understand and approach a writing task?

   1. _____

   2. _____

   3. _____

Understanding Organization

In the writing section of your handbook, you'll learn how to compose and revise a thesis statement, which is one of the most important steps in writing an academic essay. Once you find your way into your paper and begin a first draft, your handbook offers advice on writing introductions and conclusions as well as forming paragraphs that are well developed and sequential. Some handbooks show a sample student paper as it progresses through all of the stages of revision—from first to final draft. Although some students say that they don't read parts of this section unless their teacher assigns it, the information on these pages may aid you in building your thinking and expression.

You've no doubt written dozens of papers before coming to college. Were you taught somewhere along the way that there is a standard structure for every paper—an introduction, three paragraphs of explanation or support, and a conclusion? That structure will serve you well as a basic underlying foundation, but your instructor will probably be looking for something more sophisticated from your academic writing.

■ **EXERCISE 3.3: Moving Beyond the Five-Paragraph Model**
What are the common parts of a letter, a research paper, an essay test, or an essay?

Now check the contents of your handbook for information about organizing and formatting a paper. What different models does your handbook offer for organizing different kinds of writing tasks?

ACTIVITY: FINDING THE THESIS

Pick two or three writing samples—they can be newspaper or magazine articles, or classmates' writing—and identify the thesis statement in each one. What features do these sentences have that make them theses statements? Now look at the definition in your handbook for a thesis statement. Compare that definition to the features you've used to determine what makes a thesis statement. Are there differences? Or are the definitions fairly similar? Look at the sample thesis statements in the handbook to see if they fit the criteria the handbook itself has established.

Understanding Style

Most handbooks provide advice and guidance about writing style—choosing the right words, using sentences of varied lengths and structures, avoiding jargon and biased language, and more. For an easy way to improve your writing, read these sections whether or not your instructor assigns them. Good writing style means both that your writing is correct and that it has a voice—a distinct flavor that identifies it as your own.

Understanding Editing and Formatting

The last tasks that you will need to undertake before you hand in a paper are a final editing, proofreading, and formatting. Never rely on software grammar and spellcheck programs to proofread your paper; you need to check your paper carefully yourself before turning it in. There is nothing that annoys a professor more than a paper that has clearly been through a spellcheck but not proofed by its writer: *There* will substitute for *They're* and *two* for *too* too many times.

Your instructor may not spend too much time correcting your grammar. You're a college student, after all. But your instructor will probably use a set of common abbreviations to mark your most common errors. We'll spend much more time talking about grammatical issues in the last section of this chapter, but take the time now to find the editing and proofreading guide in your handbook. This guide will probably appear at the back (although sometimes in the front) of the book.

■ EXERCISE 3.4: Understanding What Those Symbols Mean

Find the following abbreviations in your handbook's guide to editing symbols. (These may also be called *revision symbols, copyediting symbols,* or *proofreading symbols.*) Write down what the symbol means, and the page numbers in the handbook where additional help with this problem can be found.

1. *coh* _____   Page numbers _____

2. *dm* _____   Page numbers _____

3. *frag* _____   Page numbers _____

4. *sub*_____   Page numbers _____

5. *//*_____   Page numbers _____

Finally, before you turn in your first paper, check your hand-book for formatting conventions. Ask your professor to confirm that this is what he or she wants as well—do you need a separate title page? Where should your name appear? Do you need a heading on each page? Often instructors have particular ideas about document design, and getting it right is important.

Research

Planning your approach to a writing assignment involves not only picking a topic and learning how to organize your paper, but also deciding whether or not you will need to do research about your subject (that is, whether or not your assignment requires a *research component*). The research section of your handbook contains useful information for each stage of planning your paper, including how to refine your topic, find and evaluate reliable sources, and integrate that source material into your paper in the form of quotations, summaries, and paraphrases.

To allow your readers to find additional material about your topic—as well as to avoid the possibility of plagiarism—you will be required to document the sources that you used both in the text of your essay and in a bibliography or Works Cited page. Documentation styles are determined by the major professional organizations in each discipline. The Modern Language Association (MLA), for example, defines the documentation style used most frequently in literature, languages, and the humanities; the American Psychological Association (APA) defines the style used in most social sciences. As a result, documentation style differs from one discipline to another. You won't use the same citation and documentation format for an English class as you would for a mechanical engineering course, for example. You'll want to find out from your professor what documentation format he or she wants for research papers—and you'll want to ask your professors in other courses as well. Never assume that one size fits all.

You also need to know that there is a specific format for every kind of source material—books, newspapers, magazines journals, and (most complicated of all) online sources. Just listing a URL (or web page address) in parentheses following your use of material from a website, for instance, is not appropriate in a college or professional paper. View your handbook as your map—and it is an absolutely essential map—for navigating through the research and documentation process.

One of the most challenging issues in college writing today is plagiarism. You may have every good intention of never plagiarizing, but you need to know exactly how to integrate source material into your paper. This may be the best advice we can provide: read the section of your handbook about plagiarism. Study the examples. Make sure you understand how to cite sources in your text itself, how to paraphrase, summarize and quote material, and how to document your sources at the end of your paper. Your college career may depend on it.

In the appendix to this book, you'll find a complete sample student research paper. This sample paper is annotated to show you how to use your handbook to find solutions for common problems associated with writing and formatting research papers.

■ EXERCISE 3.5: Finding Answers to Common Questions About Research

1. Does your handbook include a numbered list or directory of the different kinds of bibliographic entries within APA, MLA, and other citation styles?

_____

2. Does your handbook categorize the entries in this directory into groups? If so, what are these groups?

_____

3. What citation or documentation style is required for your composition course? What styles are required for research papers in each of your other classes? (If you don't know, ask your professors.)

_____

4. Is there a difference between citing an electronic copy of an article from a library database and citing a web page ? On what pages in your handbook do you find these two models?

5. On what page of your handbook can you find information about parenthetical documentation?

6. Is it considered plagiarism if you put someone else's thinking into your own words and don't include the original author's name? Where does your handbook talk about this?

7. Turn to the sample research paper in your handbook and look at the bibliography (or Works Cited page). In what order is the list arranged?

8. Flip through the paper itself and look for sets of parentheses, and then flip back to the paper's bibliography. What do you notice?

9. Do the different disciplinary documentation styles (APA, MLA, CSE, etc.) handle in-text citations differently? Does your hand-book provide a model for each of these?

10. How do you punctuate a quotation, and how do you cite it at the end of a sentence?

Grammar and Punctuation

For some students, problems with grammar and punctuation feel like speed bumps on the road to writing well; for others, these issues seem more like a full-scale road block. Many things in grammar are related, so knowing only bits and pieces can sometimes be more confusing than understanding general rules. For example, where you put a comma can depend on a number of different factors, including:

- whether you have more than one prepositional phrase in a row (which means you need to know what a preposition is, and what a prepositional phrase is)
- whether your sentence begins with a dependent clause or an independent clause
- whether you are using a coordinating conjunction between two main clauses
- whether you are using several words or phrases in a list

And you thought you just needed to put a comma wherever you need to create a . . . *pause* in the flow of your sentence!

Because novice writers often get caught in the complex web of grammar, they can get discouraged and frustrated. Perhaps this is the reason some students leave their handbook unopened and unread. If you find the grammar section of your handbook confusing, then the best way for you to find the information you need is to start with what you know. If you know the parts of a sentence (adjectives, adverbs, verbs, nouns), move on to the next level—clauses, and what kinds of clauses make up a sentence. Then skip ahead to something else that you already know—let's say you're familiar with which pronoun case to use in a sentence, but you sometimes get confused as to whether to use *I* or *me*. You would then review the chapter on pronoun case to fill in the gaps.

Most handbooks include one or more chapters covering grammar basics. (In fact, the first handbooks were simply handbooks of grammar—that's all they covered!) These basics may include a review of the parts of speech, an overview of the different types of sentences, an inventory of the major parts that work together to create sentences (for example, phrases and clauses). If you find you have trouble remembering some of the terminology (what's the difference between a *conjunction* and a *preposition*?), you'll find that the grammar basics chapter will quickly bring you back up to speed. Sometimes this grammar basics chapter may be called something similar—like "sentence types and patterns" or "parts of speech." Find this section in your handbook and tab it for future reference!

Answering the questions below will not only help you feel more comfortable with the grammar and punctuation section of your handbook, but will also help you get a head start on finding answers to a few common writing and editing questions many students face in college.

■ **EXERCISE 3.6: Getting Familiar with Grammar and Punctuation**

1. Are you familiar with the mnemonic word FANBOYS? If so, where would you look in the grammar section to find a list of these words? If not, think about this: What do the words for, and, nor, but, or, yet, and so have in common?

   _____

   _____

2. What is a tense shift? Where would you look for this in your handbook?

   _____

   _____

3. Where would you look in your handbook for help if you have difficulty with –ed endings?

   _____

   _____

4. Does your handbook provide a list of transitional words? If so, where is it?

   _____

   _____

5. What is an independent clause? Where would you find information about independent clauses in your handbook?

   _____

   _____

6. What are subordinating conjunctions? Can you find a list of these in your handbook? If so, where?

_____

_____

7. Is there a difference between a run-on sentence and a fused sentence? What is the difference between a fused sentence and a comma splice? In what section of your handbook can you find these definitions?

_____

_____

8. Can you find a handy chart that lists rules for using (or not using) commas?

_____

_____

9. Where does your handbook discuss parallelism? What are some signals that words in a sentence might not be parallel?

_____

_____

10. Does your handbook include a list of common abbreviations? Where is it?

_____

_____

Most handbook publishers provide grammar and usage drill exercises on their composition websites. If you are having trouble with any specific issues, go to the website and do the exercises there. Practicing now will prevent years of repeating the same mistakes with grammar over and over again.

What Help Does My Handbook Provide for Non-Native Speakers of English?

Most handbooks offer a special section titled "ESL" (an abbreviation for "English as a Second Language"), "Background for Multilingual Writers," or "Standard English for Academic Purposes." These sections provide detailed information about issues that non-native English speakers find most troublesome: verb forms and articles (*a, an, the*); pronouns; idioms or common phrases; word order within sentences; and more. Some of these grammar issues are also troublesome for *native* speakers—and these sections are very thorough and generally very straightforward, so sometimes reading about a grammar issue in the ESL section can be a great help. For instance, if you have difficulty with subject-verb agreement or tend to omit verb endings as you write, you might explore the ESL section for extended examples and explanations.

Grammar, however, is only a one part of the ESL section of a handbook. Other assistance for multilingual writers may include a discussion of cultural differences in writing style and expectations concerning how an academic essay should be organized.

Regardless of where you look in your handbook for grammar help, the most important resource for learning grammar is your own work. Comb your drafts for mistakes and—with your trusty handbook by your side—learn to catch the errors yourself. As you gain experience and practice, you'll be surprised at how helpful the grammar section of your handbook can be.

4

How Can My Handbook Help Me Succeed in Composition— and Beyond?

Maybe your handbook won't really make writing *easier*, but it can help with each stage of the writing process. Writing well takes time and practice, and no textbook or handbook can do that for you. But we do know there are common places where you might have difficulties: coming up with a good topic, revising a paper in response to a teacher's comments, and formatting a formal research paper. Your handbook can also be a good guide for writing papers in your other classes. Although your college handbook is not meant to replace your writing class and a good teacher, you'll find that using it can help you not only to understand what to do when you begin a writing assignment, but also to learn how to revise and edit your work.

ACTIVITY: WHAT WORRIES ME?

Take a moment to write down some concerns you have about writing in college. Consider how many times you remember getting stuck or having issues with writing projects in the past. For example, have you had difficulty finding a topic, or narrowing the topic once you've settled on it? Do you worry about what sources you should use? Are you concerned about how to form an argument? Do you find the research process somewhat intimidating?

After you've written a list of your concerns, go to the detailed table of contents in your handbook and find two or three sections in the book where each item on your list might be addressed. Discovering some of the multiple uses of your handbook (and applying the information you find) can make the task of writing in college seem less intimidating.

If you think of your handbook as a reference to use when checking grammar or documenting sources, you're only half right. As we explored in Chapter 3, handbooks actually cover all phases of the writing and composing processes. If you refer to your handbook at the beginning of a writing project (instead of waiting to open it until you are proofreading your final copy), you'll find that it will open up the planning and drafting process for you, and provide support throughout the experience of developing and revising a paper. Handbooks offer answers to frequently asked questions about writing, and finding the answers before you begin—making them part of your consciousness every time you write—will save time as you proceed through your first assignment. Some of these questions appear in Exercise 4.1.

■ EXERCISE 4.1: Frequently Asked Questions

Here is a list of questions students often ask about college writing. Answer each with Yes or No, and then look up the answers or recommendations in your handbook:

Y   N   1. Can I use *I* or *you* in a formal academic paper?

Y   N   2. Is it OK to use a popular magazine as a source for my research paper?

Y   N   3. Am I supposed to state my own opinion in my writing, or am I supposed to be completely objective?

Y   N   4. Do I have to footnote every single quote I use in my paper?

Y   N   5. Is it OK to use a source I found on the Web?

Understanding an Assignment

Sometimes college teachers provide thorough, detailed explanations of writing assignments. In other cases, they may concisely announce to the class that a 1,000-word "analytical essay" is due in two weeks. Regardless of how much detail you are given at the beginning, the first step you can take toward a successful paper is to be sure you understand exactly what an assignment is asking you to do.

First, let's look at a few assignment descriptions that some students might find confusing.

Sample Assignment #1
Write a definition of an abstract term that holds a deep meaning for you or one that holds conflicting meanings in different contexts. Some examples would be to explore the meaning of "pride," "education," or "freedom."

In Sample Assignment #1, the teacher assumes that students will understand that they will be writing an essay rather than a few sentences. The approach is expository, meaning that students are asked to present information and analyze it.

To clarify the assignment, you probably want to find answers to the following questions:

- Does the use of "you" in the assignment description imply that I can use first person "I" in this essay?
- If I don't use "I," how can I use my own experience for examples? Should the essay be written as a story (or narrative)?
- Even though most writing assignments allow for some degree of creativity, how much research might be involved for this paper? Am I supposed to research on my own, as if this were a research assignment?
- Is this a short or average length essay of approximately 500 words or something twice that size?
- Will I receive a grade on the first draft?

Because the topic is broad, you may need to consult your handbook for suggestions on narrowing a topic. You should know that sometimes teachers want an assignment to be a little open-ended. They expect you to ask questions and think critically. Teachers expect you to use your handbook for common writing issues such as forming a thesis, avoiding logical fallacies, creating interesting introductions, and organizing your essay effectively.

In Assignment #1, you will probably recognize that definition is the key word. If you look up *definition* in your handbook's index, you may discover more about how definitions work and how to effectively compose one. You may learn, for example, that definitions often begin by listing a term's distinguishing features. You might discover, further, that a definition essay often begins with a standard or common definition of a word that is then qualified or added to in unexpected ways. And you might learn that definition can also be used as a persuasive strategy, particularly when you want to challenge the way a word is used or defined by someone else. Simply by looking up one word in a handbook—*definition*—you can begin to tease out some ideas that will help you get started, generate ideas, and expand on your initial response to the assignment.

Now let's look at another sample assignment:

Sample Assignment #2
Write a report on the Six Nations of the Iroquois and how their approach to democracy influenced the American system of government.

Many of the same questions we explored for Assignment #1 also apply to Assignment #2. You need to be sure you understand the expectations for a particular context and level of formality. And you need to have a sense of audience (public? academic? specialized?) and genre (formal essay? personal narrative?) in order to begin to map out an appropriate plan and strategy. In this case, you want to be careful not to make the mistake of assuming that a "report" will be a simple summary. The word "influenced" suggests that this assignment will require a persuasive approach because you will be doing more than just writing a list of similarities between the two systems of democracy. You will need to take your essay further and explain *how* the Six Nations of the Iroquois served as a model for the American democratic system. In this case, you might want to begin by thinking about causes and effects. First, you'd want to analyze the Iroquois approach to democracy (the historical cause) and then you'd want to show how their approach influenced the U.S. system (the historical effect).

Consult your handbook for suggestions on writing a persuasive essay. Many handbooks have extensive sections on argument and persuasion, offering a range of models you might want to use to help break down a specific kind of argument (like cause–effect) and organize an effective persuasive case using a specific strategy. You might also benefit from reading about composing a thesis, writing an introduction, organizing your essay, and providing support for your position.

Sample Assignment #3 — "Engaging in a Public Debate"

You will write a research paper of 1,500 words, citing at least 5–10 sources (include a range of sources, including books, journal articles, and newspapers). Make sure that your essay is in MLA format.

In the assignment description, the words "public debate" are a significant clue that your paper is going to be an argumentative paper on an issue about which many people have and express strong opinions. With this in mind, consult your handbook on how to approach writing an argument. You may wish to read the sample paper included in the "research" section of your handbook and trace the pattern of development from paragraph to paragraph.

You may also want to check for information on relating to a specific audience, avoiding logical fallacies (if your handbook includes them), developing a clear method of organization, and creating a conclusion that accomplishes more than merely summarizing the essay's main ideas.

The fourth sample writing assignment shown here is an example of a thorough assignment description. Notice all the cues the instructor provides and use those cues to help inform and frame your approach to the assignment. Once again, checking in with your handbook early and often in the planning and drafting stages will help you develop a more effective response to the assignment. It may even save you some time and effort later!

Sample Assignment #4— Interviewing a Writer

ENGLISH 111—SECTION JA
Professor P. Longman
Suggested length: 4-6 pages
[1] First draft due: April 16, 2007
[2] Final draft due: April 30, 2007

Throughout this semester, we have listened to the voices of many different writers: from the relaxed and playful to the refined and carefully organized. Each of these writers offers us a unique look into the mind of the professional author.

This major paper follows that pattern and asks you, as a student of writing, to carefully examine the [3] voice and self-reflection of a professional writer. To do so, you will conduct a formal interview with this person. You may choose someone from your department—a published professor, for instance, or a graduate student working on a thesis/dissertation—or someone from another department whose work interests you. You might even choose someone from outside of the academy: a minister, reporter, novelist, scientist, blogger, etc. Provided that the individual employs writing as a part of his or her professional life, I am willing to accept interviews from a wide range of sources.

1. This instructor is providing a due date for the rough draft. Sometimes teachers want students to bring 2–3 copies of this draft to share with a peer group. In other cases, they will ask students to share one-on-one with their peers in class, then collect only the final versions for a grade.

2. If your teacher lists a final due date only, then you may want to plan ahead and visit your instructor during his or her office hours to discuss your draft.

3. The idea of "voice" will have been covered in class, but if you need to review, it's not what your handbook covers under "passive and active voice." (That's a different use of the term *voice* than what this assignment is intended to address.) Instead, it relates to the persona of the author and how the writer shows readers his or her personality. Although *ethos* is not exactly the same concept as *voice,* scanning the first few pages of the writing section as well as exploring the definition of *ethos* in your handbook will help.

The first step in this project is to choose an interviewee (subject to my approval). Although you may conduct the interview by phone or email, I prefer face-to-face interviews, so keep this in mind as you review possibilities. Once you have chosen someone to interview, I would like you to narrow down your interests to a single research topic, around which you will center your line of questioning. We will discuss these research topics during class, and a few sample topics appear on the back of this handout. (Note: Asking for a writing sample will help you focus in on questions relevant to the writer at hand.) Remember that people have busy lives, so you need to schedule the interview a couple weeks in advance.

Once you have selected an interviewee and formulated a list of questions, conduct the interview and begin organizing an essay around your findings. I do not want a simple transcript of the interview. [4] Instead, I would like you to use salient comments and quotes *from* the interview as a means of exploring your research topic and developing a clear argument. [5] You are encouraged (but not required) to incorporate ideas from the essays we have read.

As you will use a number of sources in writing this essay, it is necessary to attach a properly formatted

4. Here the teacher explains that the paper should be presented as a formal essay rather than in Question/Answer format. To extend this point, a topic approach may be more appropriate than a chronological approach following the sequence of the interview questions.

5. Explore the writing or rhetoric parts of your handbook to discover strategies for writing a persuasive essay. You might also benefit from reading about composing a thesis, writing an introduction, organizing your essay, and providing support.

works cited page to the final draft. In particular, you must provide me with means to contact the individual you interviewed—I will be checking your sources carefully, so take time to document these correctly. [6]

Finally, although you are receiving this assignment several weeks before the due date, do not take that as an invitation to ignore its import. Setting up and conducting an interview takes considerable time and effort; transcribing and assimilating the subsequent information demands even more! Contact me early and stay in contact throughout the process.

6. This is an explicit direction to use sources and provide a Works Cited page. You will need to look up how to cite the interview itself as well as how to cite other published works you may be using in your paper.

■ **EXERCISE 4.2: Understanding an Assignment**

1. For Sample Assignment 4, "Interviewing a Writer," you are asked to conduct *primary* as well as *secondary* research. Look up both terms in the index or in the research section of your handbook. How does your handbook differentiate these two terms?

_____

_____

_____

2. The assignment asks you to create a "Works Cited" page. The inclusion of a "Works Cited" page is specific to a particular citation style. Which one?

_____

3. Can you identify at least two major differences between APA and MLA citation and documentation style?

_____

_____

ACTIVITY: MAKE A WRITING CALENDAR

Your professor has handed out a course syllabus. Take a few minutes at the beginning of the course to annotate it with reminders to use your handbook.

- On the day of the first writing assignment, write yourself a reminder to review the sections on pre-writing in your handbook.
- If your instructor asks you to bring your draft to class for peer review, write a reminder to read applicable sections of your handbook on peer review or revision a day or two before this will happen.
- If your syllabus includes a research paper, annotate the weeks before the due date, noting which parts of the handbook you will need to refer to that week. (Make sure you understand which documentation format your professor requires, and use the section of your handbook that provides guidance for that style—MLA, APA, CSE, or CMS.) These might include sections on
  - choosing a topic,
  - writing a thesis,
  - evaluating sources,
  - creating a bibliography or "works cited" page, or
  - formatting your paper.

Responding to Feedback

If you received a paper back from your teacher with a circle around a comma, // marks, a *W* next to one section and the word *frag* next to another, would you know how to decipher these comments? Or how to respond to them?

When students receive their essays back from an instructor, sometimes they don't know how to interpret the annotations and abbreviations teachers use to mark papers. Teachers can, of course, invent their own shortcuts and grading terminology, but quite often their notations follow the same format your handbook uses. Look at the page of *revision symbols* (sometimes called *proofreading* or *editing symbols*), which you will probably find near the back or the front of your handbook. This page comprises a list of abbreviations that instructors most often use in their marginal comments.

■ **EXERCISE 4.3: Understanding Feedback**

Using the Revision Symbols page in your own handbook, look up information from the teacher's comments in the following excerpt from a student's paper. (NOTE: A complete annotated version of this paper appears in the Appendix of this book.)

> According to Ann Coulter, "The embryonic stem-cell researchers have produced nothing. They have treated nothing. They have not begun one human clinical trial" (Coulter). This statement is true, but has
>
> // a few holes in her argument. The major reason embryonic stem cells have not treated anything is because federal funding has been limited. Also, any research that has
>
> W been done has been done with limited cell bands to work with. Not to mention that embryonic stem cell research has only been
>
> frag funded since 2001.

1. What is the instructor suggesting by circling the source citation here?

   _____

2. What does the symbol the instructor uses here (//) mean? Based on the information in your handbook, how might this problem be corrected?

   _____

3. What does the letter W mean? Based on the information in your handbook, how might this problem be corrected?

   _____

4. What does *frag* mean? Based on the information in your handbook, how might this problem be corrected?

_____

Getting a good grade on your next paper—not to mention enjoying the process of writing it—depends on many variables. Although correcting grammar errors and editing your paper is important, working on the substance of your paper should be your main goal. In fact, lack of substantial support for a thesis may be the most frequent error teachers see in their students' writing. For example, statements in the paragraph above need more detail. Use the checklists below as a guide for responding to feedback and revising your essay. You can use the nearby checklists, along with your handbook, when you are responding to feedback and revising your paper.

CHECKLIST: REVISING

Review the appropriate writing process sections of your handbook, and think about the following questions:

- ❏ Is the structure and organization of my essay clear? Do the points I make follow logically, and are there clear transitions from one to the next?
- ❏ Does each paragraph support my thesis?
- ❏ Does the topic sentence of each paragraph relate to one of the goals of my paper?
- ❏ Are my arguments written persuasively?
- ❏ Does my writing avoid generalizations, support my main ideas, and develop substantive support for my thesis?

CHECKLIST: RESEARCH

Review the appropriate research sections of your handbook, and think about the following questions:

- ❏ Do I cite my sources in the correct format?
- ❏ Have I inserted any quotations without attaching them to a signal phrase?

❏ Have I relied too much on quotations and paraphrasing?
❏ Have I formatted my bibliography or works cited page correctly?

Writing an Essay Exam

We often don't think about responding to essay exams when we think about college writing—but in fact, writing an in-class essay exam can be one of the most stressful composition projects in a college career. The occasion requires you to remember subject matter that may be new to you, to be able to call up specific information from memory, and to organize and compose a well-written draft in a short amount of time. Everything your handbook says about academic writing applies to the essay exam as well: provide supporting detail for your main points; use some kind of organizational strategy so your paper has a shape and a reader can follow your train of thought; give credit to the authors of the ideas and concepts you use. Beyond that, the rhetorical occasion of the impromptu essay exam presents some specific challenges that your handbook may help you cope with.

Your handbook will probably remind you to

- Learn what to expect.
- Study early and often.
- Anticipate possible questions.
- Make a plan.
- Revise and proofread.

Beyond this good advice, a handbook can also help you better understand the expectations and conventions of different academic disciplines. For an essay exam in a history class, for example, you might expect to be asked to provide historical context, chronological evidence (when things happened relative to one another, as opposed to providing specific dates), and causal analysis (how developments in agriculture, for example, led to population growth). In an art class, on the other hand, you might be expected to demonstrate in an essay exam that you understand and can apply specific terms like *surrealism* or *expressionism*. You may not be able to refer to your handbook during the exam itself, but spending a little time with it the night before can help you think through the process of writing the exam essay, and may just save you some stress when you do sit down to write.

Overall, your handbook is a good resource for writing not only in your composition course, but for every single piece of writing you will be asked to do in college—including writing for other courses, or writing essay exams. It can also help you understand what your professors are asking you to do, and how to respond to their feedback.

5

How Can My Handbook Help Me Write a Research Paper?

Many first-year writing courses include an assignment for a research paper. And if you are not asked to write a research paper in your composition course, you almost certainly will be asked to do so in one or more of your other college courses. If you think of your handbook as your travel guide on the road to writing well, then what would you expect your travel guide to tell you about "research-paper-land"? Would it be an easy commute on the information highway? Would it be like climbing Mount Everest . . . or nothing like either one? Without a map for writing a good research paper, it's natural to be confused by all the twists and turns, busy intersections, multiple destinations, multiple opinions from locals giving you their advice, and confusing signs along the way.

Even experts get lost on their way to finishing a research project. In fact, every research paper assignment—no matter how small—requires a lot of thought, preparation, and attention to detail. In fact, so much can go wrong with a research assignment that sometimes it seems impossible to do everything well. The key is to plan everything step by step.

And then expect to hit some detours. In fact, good research often leads writers to adapt, adjust, or even abandon their original ideas and hypotheses. Research is like exploration: you may find new things you didn't expect, take a different path than the one you originally mapped out, and find yourself in a different place than you set out to discover. You need to remain open to new ideas, willing to revise and reshape your assumptions, and flexible enough to allow yourself room to change your mind. Many handbooks will offer you a detailed example of a research project as it develops. Take a look at how other students and other writers have approached the research project, and think about how you can learn from their experience and adapt it to your own interests and situation.

Even though some of the steps in the research process overlap, and you may have to backtrack now and then, choosing the right topic for the right assignment is the best way to start.

Choosing a Topic

The first necessary step is to read your assignment carefully. Can you choose your own topic or must you choose from a list your teacher provided for the class? Who is your audience for the paper? Regardless of the context and situation, you need to pick something that interests you enough to spend the next several weeks reading about it. A good paper not only engages your mind but also your emotions.

ACTIVITY: FINDING A TOPIC

Sometimes your instructor will give you a specific topic for your research paper, but often you will be left to discover a subject for your paper yourself. How do you begin? Well, try using some of the following questions to help you find a topic that engages both your mind and your passion.

- What is bugging me about _____?
- What would I like to change about _____ (politically, socially, educationally, culturally)?
- What really makes me want to stand up and shout "That's wrong" or "That's right"?
- What have I always wanted to explore?
- Is there an issue that someone in my family is facing that I'd like to research?

Once you are confident that you've found a topic that interests you, the next step is to explore the wealth of general resources that are available on the subject. As your instructor will tell you, however, before you actually create a thesis statement or start writing your paper, you will need to narrow your topic and get clear about the point(s) you plan to make to your readers.

Most handbooks include a list of general reference sources that may help you identify and narrow a research topic. Look for your specific discipline or subject area, and then search within that for encyclopedias, indexes, bibliographies, and databases that will help to begin and fuel your search process.

■ **EXERCISE 5.1: Narrowing Your Topic**
Use the navigational aids in your handbook to find answers to the following questions. Provide section or page numbers.

1. Which part of the Research section of my handbook provides advice on narrowing a topic?

   _____

2. Are there other places in my handbook besides the research paper section that offer advice on narrowing a topic?

   _____

3. Where does my handbook offer advice about using websites in research?

   _____

4. Does my handbook suggest any specific resources as good starting places for exploring and narrowing a topic? Where is the list of these resources located?

   _____

5. Does my handbook publisher offer online access to research resources for my topic? How do I know that?

   _____

Online Research

Cutting and pasting from online sources seems so simple—but be aware that instructors notice when students use Google, Wikipedia, or other web-based search engines or sources to find information and then cut and paste it into an essay. Even if you use quotation marks and cite your sources to prevent plagiarism, the "cut and paste" method of compiling a paper from generic websites may turn out to be lethal to your GPA and your academic credibility. Assembling a paper this way is plagiarism, and plagiarism is an academic crime of the worst order.

Although the Internet is a wonderful tool for finding general resources, your teacher expects you to conduct college-level research. Probably the best place to start is your library's databases.

Most handbooks will include one or more chapters on finding and evaluating online sources. Take some time to see what your handbook offers before you start plugging keywords into Google, and you just may find that the online research process becomes more manageable and effective. The challenge today is not in how much information you can find. The Web has made a virtual universe of information available to anyone with an Internet connection. Rather, the real challenge in online research is to find information that is actually useful—relevant, credible, current, and appropriate to your writing situation, your audience, and your topic.

The first thing you may learn is that not all online searches take you to the same place. Google, for example, will link you to open source (public) web pages, many of which are commercial, biased, and uneven in quality. In contrast, an online search through your library's catalog, or through a database like Academic Search Premier or LexisNexis, will direct you to high-quality, peer-reviewed, academic research sources. These databases, unlike Google, link to closed sites that your library or university has paid money to subscribe to. Your handbook can offer you a wealth of specific guidance on online and database search strategies that will help you make the most of your search time. Remember, it's not important to find 17,000 sources on your topic: It's important to find the 5 or 6 best ones for your purpose and your audience!

Let's explore what your handbook says about conducting online and Web-based research.

■ **EXERCISE 5.2: Researching Sources**

Check your handbook to answer the following questions.

1. What advice does my handbook offer, if any, on using *key-words* or *library subject headings*?

_____

_____

_____

2. What is the difference between a *bibliography* and a *bibliographic index*?

_____

_____

_____

3. What are *electronic, full-text databases* and what does my handbook say about them?

_____

_____

_____

4. Does my handbook offer advice on *conducting interviews* as part of a research assignment?

_____

_____

_____

5. Does my handbook recommend any specific online sources? If so, which ones?

_____

_____

_____

Evaluating Sources

If you find something useful on the Internet, in a magazine, or in a book, how do you know whether or not the information comes from a reliable source? If anyone with an Internet connection can publish professional-looking web pages, how are you supposed to filter out reliable, credible research from the welter of internet noise, chat, opinion, and misinformation? This is one of the most difficult parts of conducting effective college research today. In recent years, handbooks have added more and more coverage to help provide strategies and techniques for evaluating sources, especially online sources.

ACTIVITY: EVALUATING SOURCES

Most handbooks identify a set of core criteria that apply to any research sources, print or electronic: currency (timeliness), relevance, credibility, and authority. Take a moment to find your handbook's chapter or section on evaluating sources, and make a note of the key criteria it identifies. Write down a brief definition of each term and sketch out a brief checklist you can use when you are sorting through your sources.

■ EXERCISE 5.3: Doing Research

Identify where answers to the following questions can be found in your handbook. Provide the section number or page number in each case.

1. What are *abstracts* and how can they help me?

_____

2. What is the difference between a *professional journal* and a *magazine*?

_____

3. What is the difference between an *in-text citation* and a *works cited* or *bibliographic entry*?

_____

4. How can I tell if a website has reliable information?

_____

5. How can I evaluate an author's credibility?

_____

6. How important is it to have recent information for an academic paper? What qualifies as "recent" data—does it differ depending on the topic?

_____

7. What databases, dictionaries, indexes, or kinds of sources are most appropriate for academic writing? Does this differ based on the topic?

_____

8. Does my handbook offer a checklist to help me evaluate sources?

_____

9. What advice does my handbook offer about using the library?

_____

10. Does my handbook provide a directory of models for citing print source? For citing electronic sources?

_____

Plagiarism

Some teachers are very specific about what constitutes plagiarism, and they reinforce what they mean by "academic honesty" throughout the term. Others, however, take for granted that students will read and understand what plagiarism is by reading the applicable sections of the handbook.

You are probably very much aware of the more explicit forms of plagiarism: Internet paper mills, house paper files, friends—you know someone who has done it. But what about the more subtle and invasive forms of plagiarism? Where do you draw the line between what is fair, ethical, and acceptable in academic work and what is not? And who gets to decide?

There are not always clear and concise answers to these questions. All research builds on the ideas and words of the past. No idea is ever truly "original," even though originality and creativity are highly valued in academic settings. Even experienced authors sometimes find themselves in embarrassing situations when another author accuses them of using ideas without citing their sources. We all understand that plagiarism is a bad thing and practicing it can get you into serious trouble in a college setting. So how can a handbook help you avoid such trouble?

Nearly every handbook today will devote a chapter or more to explaining what plagiarism is and how it can be avoided. Take a moment to look up *plagiarism* in the index and table of contents for your handbook, and use the questions in the following exercise to deepen your understanding of this highly charged topic.

■ **EXERCISE 5.4: What Is Plagiarism and How Can I Avoid It?**
Use your handbook to answer the following questions.

1. How does my handbook define plagiarism? Would it be plagiarism to cite three or more words in a row from another source without using quotation marks?

   _____

   _____

   _____

2. What is the difference between paraphrasing and quoting?

   _____

   _____

   _____

3. When I paraphrase a source, do I still need to cite it?

   _____

   _____

   _____

4. What suggestions does my handbook provide about avoiding plagiarism?

_____

_____

_____

5. What suggestions does my handbook provide on introducing or incorporating quotes?

_____

_____

_____

Documentation

Your handbook probably devotes more pages to documentation than to any other single topic. In addition, the multitude of different kinds of documentation formats can be confusing. Students often ask, "Why can't they all be the same?" Although that would make life easier for professors and students, the formats are relatively standardized according to discipline. Your science course will require a different research paper format than your psychology instructor or your religion class. Because of these differences, you will need to pay attention to which format your teacher requires. If you're not sure, ask your instructor.

Each format also has multiple forms of citing information in the text of the paper as well as in the bibliography, including different ways to cite newspaper articles, journal articles, Internet sources, books, and other sources. In fact, the rapid growth of electronic sources has spurred an explosion in the forms of citations necessary to document and cite such sources. Check the research section of your handbook to view the list of source formats for each style.

While handbooks include many sample citations and bibliography entries, the most important thing you can do is learn to understand the underlying pattern. When you cut through all of the complexity and detail, documenting sources is actually rather simple: provide just enough information so that your reader can retrace your steps and find the same sources you found when you did your research.

If you rush into the documentation chapters in your handbook trying to find one particular type of source at the last minute, you are likely to be frustrated. But if, on the other hand, you take a few minutes now to learn how your handbook works and how it organizes its documentation coverage, you will save far more time—and produce a more accurate bibliography—later.

■ **EXERCISE 5.5: Formatting a Research Paper Citation**
Use the MLA guide in the research section of your handbook to answer the following questions.

1. Is the citation below correct, based on the following database entry? If not, correct it.

   Database entry:

   LexisNexis Academic ◄————————— This is the database title.

   Copyright 2006 Nationwide News Pty Limited
   All Rights Reserved
   Sunday Telegraph (Australia) ◄——— This is the title of the newspaper
   where the article appeared.

   October 1, 2006 Sunday

   SECTION: FEATURES; Body and Soul; Pg. 10 ◄——— Note that the article appears only on one page.

   HEADLINE: STEM CELLS THE FACTS ◄— This is the title of the article.

   BYLINE: Jane Martin ◄————————— This is the author of the article.

   BODY: ◄——————————— Below this point is the text of the article.

   Stem cell research has the potential to cure several diseases. But what is it and why has it attracted so much controversy? By Jane Martin.

Citation:

```
Martin, Jane. Stem cell research has the

     potential to cure several diseases.

     But what is it and why has it

     attracted so much controversy? Stem

     Cells The Facts. (2006). http://web.

     lexis-nexis.com.proxy.usf.edu/

     universe/document?_m=aba254067b9784ee

     9499b19490c8fa69&_docnum=16&wchp=dGLb

     Vtb-zSkVA&_md5=f2d59514e8f51d15b53b7

     01301c25662
```

2. What guidance does your handbook provide concerning long URLs?

3. Introduce the following in-text quote with a signal phrase:

```
"By law, embryos may not be more than

fourteen days old" (Martin).
```

4. What do you know about the credibility of the author of this article, Jane Martin? How might you find more information about her? Does the database entry suggest that she is a researcher or a reporter?

5. Combine the two sentences below by paraphrasing the information and introducing the source:

```
"Embryonic stem cells hold a much larger

value to scientists in research. Human

embryonic stem cells are thought to have
```

much greater developmental potential than

adult stem cells" (NIH).

6. Now go to the APA section of your handbook. Create a citation for the database entry above using APA style.

7. The next source entry requires a total revision. Check the MLA portion of your Handbook on citing online government documents, and make the appropriate revisions.

NIH Stem Cell Information Home Page. In *Stem*

Cell Information [World Wide Web site].

Bethesda, MD: National Institutes of

Health, U.S. Department of Health and

Human Services, 2006 [cited Friday,

November 17, 2006] Available at

http://stemcells.nih.gov/index

APPENDIX
SAMPLE STUDENT PAPER

NOTE: The comments in the margins are common symbols your teacher might put on your paper.

The numbered annotations provide suggestions for how to use your handbook to improve your writing so that you don't keep making the same mistakes in your essays.

Learner 1

Ima Learner {1}

ENC 1101-049

March 3, 2007

Professor P. Longman{2}

Truth about Stem Cell Research

If you{3} had the chance to save a human life,
would you seize the opportunity? Or if the
governmental politics would inhibit you from saving
lives, would you fight it? That is what scientists
and researchers across the world are trying to do.
They have found that by using stem cells they can
possibly find the cure for many degenerative
diseases such as Parkinson's. However, political
intervention has stopped a lot of research funding
for stem cell study. I believe that this is unfair,
and will have a negative impact on the world. I
think that the government should stay out of this
affair and let the scientists do their job.{4} I
firmly agree with{5} using both adult and embryonic
stem cell research to find cures for major diseases
that could save thousands of lives,{6} and help
people around the world.

log

What is a stem cell? Stem cells are broken into
two different categories: adult and embryonic.
"Adult stem cells are present in all organs of the
body, whereas embryonic stem cells come from an
embryo, explains Dr. Andrew Elefanty" (Martin).{7}
The importance of adult stem cells is that they can

1. Number your pages and include a "header" with the page numbers on each page.

2. Since this is a paper requiring MLA style formatting, check your handbook for the correct order of information and spacing.

3. Check with your instructor and your handbook for guidelines on language and style for formal essays. You can look under "you" in the index for the appropriateness of whether to use a generalized "you." Some teachers ask students to avoid using (the second person pronoun) "you." Ask your teacher what he or she thinks about the opening of this essay and the appropriateness of using "you" here as well as the use of "your" in the second paragraph.

4. *log* Look in your handbook for information about logical fallacies (or faulty logic), especially in terms of overgeneralizations. The phrase "the government" implies the government of one nation, yet, a few sentences earlier, you mention "scientists and researchers across the world." If you are discussing the stem cell controversy within the U.S. (and consequently the impact that research in the U.S. has upon the rest of the world), then clarify this point by articulating it better.

5. Your introduction needs to give readers more preparation for your thesis. Sometimes the second paragraph in a research essay contains the thesis statement. Note that the next paragraph defines what adult and embryonic stem cells are, but this definition follows your thesis rather than precedes it. Because of your need to prepare your readers, you need to revise and extend your first paragraph. Look in the writing section of your handbook for information on composing introductions and in the research section for writing research papers.

6. *Circle around comma* Your handbook contains a lot of information about commas. Although it might be difficult to know which parts of it to consult for this particular question, scanning the chapter on commas will help you review what you already know; then you will be able to find what you need. In this case, you may be instinctively using a comma because you see the word "and." However, this is just two verbs (*saved* and *help*) joined by "and" rather than a series of three. A list of two does not need a comma before "and."

7. *Good use of a tag on the end of your quote.* Since this information came from an article in a library database, you don't need to cite a page number. If your paper was written in APA format, your citation style here would include the year.

become any organ from which they came. For instance, if a doctor removed cells from your liver, then those cells will become liver cells. Also, if cells were from blood they would reproduce and become blood cells. With this technology scientists have been able to help thousands of people with bone marrow transplants to help cure leukemia. "Bone marrow transplants to treat leukemia have been around for about 40 years and involve blood stem cells from bone marrow being transplanted to a recipient. The donated blood stem cells multiply and create a new blood system in the recipient" (Martin).{8} Using adult stems is a great {9} way to start curing people of once-thought of incurable diseases.{10} However, adult stem cells are not perfect. In some cases stem cells are not present in organs such as the pancreas. In order to extract stem cells from organs like the pancreas scientists have to rely on embryonic stem cells.

awk

Embryonic stem cells hold a much larger value to scientists in research. "Human embryonic stem cells are thought to have much greater developmental potential than adult stem cells" (NIH). The stem cells are undifferentiated, which means they have the potential to turn into any kind of cell in the body. First an egg must be fertilized and after six days the embryo is called a blastocyst, which is the earliest form of an embryo. "It contains a cluster

8. *Incorporate quote.* Check your handbook for use of "signal phrases" or ways of introducing quotations. Usually, teachers advise students not to drop in quotes without introducing them. Can you find other quotes in this paper that are just "dropped in"?

9. The word "great" is informal and non-specific.

10. *awk* Check the list of revision symbols on the inside cover of your book. "Awk" means "awkward"; the suggestion from your instructor is to improve your phrasing. Although not every student makes the same kinds of errors, it might help you to review your handbook's section on "Awkward Diction or Construction."

of about 30 cells, which are used in embryonic stem
cell research" (Martin). Once cells are removed from
the blastocyst they can no longer develop into human
beings. Scientists obtain these embryonic stem cells
from human embryos that aren't used in in vitro
fertilization. "By law, embryos may not be more than
fourteen days old" (Martin). Using these cells {11}
scientists hope to find what causes these cells to
develop into specialized cells like heart, lung, and
blood cells. Using embryonic stem cells is much more
effective than using their counterpart adult stem
cells. For example, only embryonic stem cells could
be taken to replace the pancreatic cells that the
adult stems could not. This process could save the
lives of persons with diabetes and who needs insulin
from the pancreas to stay alive. However, there is
much heated controversy surrounding the use of
embryonic stem cells.{12}

The argument around using embryonic stem cells
is simple: some believe that life begins at the
moment of fertilization, so using embryonic stem
cells would be murder since after removed;{13} the
cells can no longer produce a human. According to
Ann Coulter, "The embryonic stem-cell researchers
have produced nothing. They have treated nothing.
They have not begun one human clinical trial"
(Coulter){14}. This statement is true, but has a
few holes in her argument {15}. The major reason

//

11. Should a comma appear here? Check the commas section of your handbook.

12. Your paragraph builds from just providing background information to making a point. This also serves as a nice transition to your next paragraph. Please check your use of quotations; you need to paraphrase some information and add a signal phrase to others. Look to see what your handbook says about argument paragraphs and topic sentences.

13. This is an improper use of the semicolon. Look in your handbook's punctuation section for help.

14. You need a page number from her book instead of listing the author's name. When you list the author's name in the sentence, you don't need to cite it in the parentheses at the end of the paraphrase or quotation. See your handbook's MLA style guide for more information.

15. // Look up what this symbol means in the "revision guide" of your handbook. If you follow the structure of your sentence, you are saying, "This statement . . . has a few holes in her argument." The statement cannot have "holes"; her logic does. Important information in your sentence is missing due to a generalization that ignores the other complexities you mention.

Learner 4

embryonic stem cells have not treated anything is
because federal funding has been limited. Also, any
research that has been done has been done{16} with   W
limited cell bands to work with. Not to mention that
embryonic stem cell research has only been funded
since 2001.{17} Abortionists around the world say   frag
that "using human embryos is unethical, tantamount
to destroying human life" (LaPook). Even the church
is against the use of embryonic research. According
to Ms. Carol Hogan, who is one of the members of the
Catholic Conference Bishops of California, "Church
teaching is that we value life from conception to
natural death, and that includes embryos. So we
oppose the killing of embryos for their parts"
(LaPook). In her quote she says that{18} the church
values human life, from conception to natural death.
I believe that saving the life of a human is putting
value to that life. What one has to remember is that
these embryonic stem cells are not human,{19} they   CS
are just cells. No human development has taken
place. Hands have not grown, limbs have not sprouted
from the non-existent torso, and the cells do not
even have brain activity. To argue that using these
stem cells to try and find cures constitutes as
murder is ludicrous. According to Michael J. Fox
"All we're saying is if we're going to do that
[using embryonic cells]{20}, then let's use that to
help people. Let's use that to save lives" (LaPook).

16. W Look up this symbol in your handbook's "revision guide." What does "W" mean? Follow up on the information it provides.

17. *frag*

18. *Improve your wording here.*

19. CS Check the "revision symbols" list for what "CS" means in your handbook and follow up on the information.

20. Why is the writer using brackets here? Look up how to use quotations in the research section of your handbook.

Learner 5

If scientists are sacrificing embryos, at least they are furthering society that could have (a){21} outstanding impact in the future.

In conclusion, society should allow stem cells to have the potential to work. I think one of the major reasons people are against embryonic cells is because they are not educated in the area. I believe that given the chance embryonic research could and will surpass the benefits of adult stem cells in ten years or less. Motivating people to allow embryos to be used can come in the form of television ads, flyers, and maybe even television shows to show the potential. The fight against stem cell research will take years to settle, but the conflict would be easier if people are more informed about the situation.

Ima,

Although your draft is off to a good start, I think your argument needs a few more paragraphs with evidence to strengthen your position. The quotes from Michael J. Fox, Ann Coulter, and the Catholic bishop are interesting; however, these "popular" voices outweigh scientific evidence in your paper. Basically, I would like to see more support regarding the abundance of researchers you mention in your introduction.

Please check your Handbook for more information, especially concerning how to compile a "Works Cited" page. {22}

21. The words "a/an" are articles. Look up the articles "a" and "an" in your handbook.

22. Teachers don't always tell you to look in your handbook because they assume that their students will apply the information from the handbook to their papers.

Learner 6

Works Cited

Coulter, Ann. Godless: The Church of Liberalism. New
    York, June 6, 2006.{23}

LaPook, Jon. Eye on Medicine; Embryonic stem cell
    research holds tremendous promise but provokes
    just as much controversy. CBS Evening News.
    Oct. 27,{24} 2006. http://web.lexis-nexis.
    com.proxy. usf.edu/universe/document?_
    m=87c5301d369ff124c0719e76216f2041&_docnum=
    21&wchp=dGLbVtz-zSkVA&_md5=1c0f14a5ee02ea
    2c52cb84da401116b6{25}

Martin, Jane. Stem cell research has the potential
    to cure several diseases. But what is it and
    why has it attracted so much controversy?{26}
    Stem Cells The Facts. (2006).{27}
    http://web.lexis-nexis.com.proxy.usf.edu/
    universe/document?_m=aba254067b9784ee9499b19490
    c8fa69&_docnum=16&wchp=dGLbVtb-zSkVA&_
    md5=f2d59514e8 f51d15b53b701301c25662

NIH Stem Cell Information Home Page. In Stem Cell
    Information [World Wide Web site]. Bethesda,
    MD: National Institutes of Health, U.S.
    Department of Health and Human Services, 2006
    [cited Friday, November 17, 2006] Available at
    http:// stemcells.nih.gov/index {28}

23. Did your information come from a book, a website, or an article? If it is from a book, no publisher is listed and the date should not contain "June 6."

24. The number precedes the month. Check your handbook for the correct MLA citation style here.

25. This URL is too long. See your handbook for how to list URLs you found from a library database. Sometimes you may need to list the search terms and path you used. Be sure to check elsewhere in your works cited list (and in your annotated bibliography) for long URLs and fix those, too. Remember that teachers tend to mark an error one time in your paper; after that, they expect you to find the same kinds of errors yourself.

26. This is not part of the title of the article.

27. This is not the correct MLA citation style for an article you found in the library's database (in this case, LexisNexis Academic). You have a lot of missing information. See your handbook's MLA style guide for how to cite an article from a database. It may also be listed under how to cite an article that has been published online as well as in print.

28. Most of this entry is incorrect in terms of citation style. Also, check this citation for consistency (you used underlines in the above but used italics here).

Annotated Bibliography{29}

Coulter, Ann. <u>Godless: The Church of Liberalism.</u> New
York, June 6, 2006.

I used this book solely for the purpose of
getting opposing view points about stem cell
research. Most of what Ann Coulter is saying{30} in
her book is very radical and too extreme for me. She
of course{31} is a staunch conservative and her book
is the same. She gave{32} just a few points to
address in the topic. Her attitude towards abortion
and stem cell research made me think more about my
argument, {33} and how to make it some fail safe in
terms of debate. Anything she said I had to back it
with information and facts that made my argument
more factual.

LaPook, Jon. Eye on Medicine; Embryonic stem cell
research holds tremendous promise but provokes
just as much controversy. <u>CBS Evening News.</u>
Oct. 27, 2006. http://web.lexis-nexis.com.
proxy.usf.edu/universe/document?_m=87c5301d369f
f124c0719e76216f2041&_docnum=21&wchp=dGLbVtz-
zSkVA&_md5=1c0f14a5ee02ea2c52cb84 da401116b6
This site was the second most used site in my
paper. I used this mostly for the ethos{34} part of my
paper to show feelings. It was a conversation with
Michael J. Fox, and his words on stem cell research.

29. Annotated bibliographies are useful for research projects because they help you organize information as well as give your readers an overview of available resources. Look in your handbook for how to compile an annotated bibliography.

30. Your teacher may mark this phrase as "wordy" or this section as an overuse of "to be" verbs. Look both of these style issues in your handbook.

31. The phrase "of course" interrupts between the subject and verb. Check the commas chapter of your handbook.

32. When you write about something that has been written by someone else, you use present tense. Look for other parts of this paragraph that switch from present tense to past tense.

33. Apply what you learned about commas here and elsewhere in your paper.

34. Some handbooks provide students with explanations of the three rhetorical appeals: *ethos*, *pathos*, and *logos*. Check the writing section of your handbook to see what it includes about each and how you might apply these concepts to the way you think about "audience" in your papers.

Learner 8

Since he has Parkinson's it was a good tear jerker{35}
to get people to realize the possibilities. Not only
did this source give me a good person to talk about,
but it also had a lot of facts within the discussion.
This proved useful later in my paper to give it more
credibility. This source actually affected my writing
to make it more emotional and heart-driven then{36}
anything else. Which was good because a paper needs to
have that including factual data.{37}   frag

Martin, Jane. Stem cell research has the potential
        to cure several diseases. But what is it and
        why has it attracted so much controversy? Stem
        Cells The Facts. (2006).{38} http://web.lexis-
        nexis.com. proxy.usf.edu/universe/document?_
        m=aba254067b9784ee9499b19490c8fa69&_docnum=16&w
        chp=dGLbVtb-zSkVA&_md5=f2d59514e8f51d15b53b
        701301c25662{39}
        This site was used the most in my paper. I used
this site for most of my information about stem cell
research and the controversy surrounding the topic.
It explained in detail about adult stem cells and
embryonic stem cells. It also discussed their
usefulness, and the disadvantages. One of good
things about this site is that it goes into the
controversy. Most of what is being said in the news
is stated in the paper. Not only was the article
filled with information it was also very short and

35. Check your handbook for use of appropriate language and style here.

36. Check your handbook index for "then/than."

37. *frag* Look at the list of "Common Errors" or "Revision Symbols" on the front or back pages of your handbook.

38. This is not the correct MLA citation style for an article you found in the library's database (in this case, LexisNexis Academic). You have a lot of missing information. See your handbook's MLA style guide for how to cite an article from a database. It may also be listed under how to cite an article that has been published online as well as in print.

39. This URL is too long. See your handbook for how to list URLs you found from a library database. Sometimes you may need to list the search terms and path you used.

to the point. This was good when you had about ten
different articles to read through.

NIH Stem Cell Information Home Page. In *Stem Cell*
Information [World Wide Web site]. Bethesda, MD:
National Institutes of Health, U.S. Department of
Health and Human Services, 2006 [cited Friday,
November 17, 2006] Available at http://
stemcells.nih.gov/ index

This site was pretty useful{40} in terms of
information. I was looking for a non-biased site
with some information about stem cell research. It
had a really good question and answer page that
really helped me with my paper. It had loads of
definitions, and also side comments about stem cell
research. This is also a very useful source because
it is from a reliable source which makes my paper
seen more creditable. One of the good things about
this site was that it had link to various other web
sites about the topic. Different research companies
where on the home page, and other links as well.

40. Check your handbook for appropriate language. "Pretty useful" is too informal for a research paper, even when it's used in an annotated bibliography.

INDEX

Additional Titles in the WESSKA (*What Every Student Should Know About . . .*) Series:

- *What Every Student Should Know About Avoiding Plagiarism* (ISBN 0-321-44689-5)

- *What Every Student Should Know About Citing Sources with APA Documentation* (ISBN 0-205-49923-6)

- *What Every Student Should Know About Citing Sources with MLA Documentation* (ISBN 0-321-44737-9)

- *What Every Student Should Know About Creating Portfolios* (ISBN 0-205-57250-2)

- *What Every Student Should Know About Researching Online* (ISBN 0-321-44531-7)

- *What Every Student Should Know About Practicing Peer Review* (ISBN 0-321-44848-0)

- *What Every Student Should Know About Preparing Effective Oral Presentations* (ISBN 0-205-50545-7)

- *What Every Student Should Know About Reading Maps, Figures, Photographs, and More* (ISBN 0-205-50543-0)

- *What Every Student Should Know About Study Skills* (ISBN 0-321-44736-0)

- *What Every Student Should Know About Writing Across the Curriculum* (ISBN 0-205-58913-8)